Lan[illegible] nder,

Charles Read
Director of Liturgy and Worship,
Eastern Region Ministry Course and
Director of LLM Training, Diocese of Norwich

GROVE BOOKS LIMITED
RIDLEY HALL RD CAMBRIDGE CB3 9HU

Contents

Acknowledgments

I am grateful to members of the Group for the Renewal of Worship for comments on this booklet and especially to Mark Earey who went the extra mile in helping me get it ready for publication. It has two origins. It is based on PhD research I began many years ago and I am grateful to the late professor Ann Loades for being my supervisor. She helped me focus the issues around inclusive language and was a brilliantly supportive and challenging supervisor. The prior origin of this booklet lies in the Joint Liturgical Study which was produced by Viv Faull and Jane Sinclair in 1986. Jane became my liturgy teacher at theological college and was a great friend and influence. Like Ann, she is sadly missed. It was reading the booklet by Jane and Viv just as I was going off to train for ordination that got me interested in the issues which are discussed in this booklet, which I offer as a sort of thank you to the two of them—these issues have taken up a large part of my academic career ever since.

First Impression August 2024
ISSN 0144-1728
ISBN 978 1 78827 407 4

1

Is God a Boy?

Allegedly, a little girl's prayer said, 'Dear God, do you prefer boys to girls? I know you are a boy but please try to be fair.'

This story usually raises a smile or two because, when we stop and think about it, we would not say that God is male. Christians have never believed that God is male, although my experience of trying out some of the research which lies behind this booklet on non-Christian groups of academics reveals that people outside the church often do assume that the Christian God is male.

Yes the Bible—especially our English translations—does seem to speak as if God is male: there are lots of male pronouns for God and lots of labels and imagery such as calling God Lord. However, there are occasions when the Bible uses female language and imagery to talk about God and there is a very telling point in the creation story where it says that it is men and women together who reflect God's image (Gen 1.27).

Then there are pastoral issues such as these two examples which I have made up based on numerous conversations I have had with people over the years:

> Kathy was abused by her father when she was a child. When she goes to church and God is referred to as Father, this often brings back memories of this abuse. She finds it impossible not to link the word *father* with abuse.
>
> Phil grew up in a single-parent household with his mother and has never known what it is to have a human father. The language about God as Father does not bring negative feelings for him like it often does for Kathy. In fact, it does not do anything for him because he does not have any human experience to connect it with. He is now married with children himself and tries to be a good father but being the child of a father is not part of his own experience.

There are lots of people in our churches with experiences like these for whom prayers, hymns and other texts that speak of God as father do not connect with them or, worse, evoke painful memories.

Are there other ways to speak of God which we could set alongside the idea of God as father? Could we even speak of God as mother? And if we do this, are there advantages for people who do have positive experiences of the relationship with their own fathers? That is what this booklet is about. We begin with some exploration of the issues and possible ways forward (this chapter and chapters two and three). Chapters four and five explore how some denominations have responded. If you are keen to get to some practical ideas for local churches, you might want to jump straight to chapter six.

The Power of Words in Worship

We are warned in the Bible not to have meaningless disputes over words and it is sometimes said that concern about gendered language is one of those things which comes into this category. However, the Bible has other things to say about words which demonstrates their power. Apart from the strictures in the Letter of James about being careful about the language we use because words have the power to hurt, there is the theme in the creation story in Genesis 1 about words being the way in which God creates the world. Neither is it accidental that in John 1 Jesus is described as the Word, an echo of Genesis 1.

The Bible knows that words are powerful, and so paying attention to the words we use to describe God and to speak to God is important. In corporate worship it becomes even more significant, because our worship is where we declare together what we believe about the God we believe in. Here are some key factors:

- There is much truth in the suggestion that the way we use language shapes the way we think about things, even if this is not quite as straightforward as some have argued.[1] This insight could apply to many other things, not just the way we talk about God. You may like to scrutinize the worship in your church with a view to such things as how salvation is described or what images are used to describe the church.
- If we only use a small range of ways of describing God in our worship, then we are limiting God by not using the full range of images available to us in the Bible and developed in later Christian history.
- It follows from this that we are also restricting people's spirituality if we use a limited range of words for God. Not only is it more true to the Bible to use a broad range of images for God in our worship, it is also good for people's development as Christians and for their growth in prayer and spirituality.
- On top of all of this, in corporate worship we tend to repeat what we say across weeks and years, and even set it to music, so that it

sinks in very deeply indeed. This means that we need to work hard to make sure that what is sinking in is what we really want to say.

Being concerned about issues of language about gender in worship is not some passing fad, nor should it be dismissed as political correctness. It is about being biblically faithful and describing God in all the glorious diversity which the Bible does.

The Bible Speaks about God

The Bible speaks about human beings being made in the image of God, but what is that image? The Bible often uses male imagery to speak of God but that is not the whole story. The Old Testament includes imagery for God which includes inanimate objects (for example, God as rock), animals (God as bear), function (what God does, for example, redeemer) and human offices (God as king).[2] Into this last category we might put God as father—a description of God surprisingly rare in the Old Testament and just one image among many—though it is more common in the New Testament.

The Bible often uses male imagery to speak of God but that is not the whole story

Deuteronomy 32.11, for instance, refers to God as a mother bird brooding over chicks: '[God's action is] as an eagle stirs up its nest and hovers over its young.' This links back to Genesis 1.2 where the same word (here translated 'hovers') is used of God's Spirit (or possibly breath) hovering over the waters of chaos which are being ordered into creation. This imagery of God as mother bird occurs in several other places in the Old Testament and is picked up by Jesus as we will see.

Later in Deuteronomy 32, there is a reference to God giving birth to his people (Deut 32.18) in a verse which also depicts God as a rock which (or maybe who) fathers people. The image of God as midwife or nursing mother occurs elsewhere in the Old Testament too—Job 10.18 may have this in mind when it refers to God bringing Job forth from the womb. A similar image is found in Isa 66.9.

A more complex Old Testament image is that of God as wisdom personified. This is most clearly seen in Proverbs 8. In much discussion of this image of God as wisdom, it is pointed out that wisdom is personified as female (maybe because the Hebrew work *hochmah* is grammatically feminine). Many people see a connection between God personified as wisdom and John's gospel describing Jesus as the Word.[3]

So the Old Testament employs a range of imagery for God within which 'father' is quite rarely used. Feminine imagery is used within this range. What about ways of describing Jesus? Alongside the possibilities opened up by the connection between wisdom and word discussed above, a more obvious example of feminine imagery comes in Luke 13.34 and Matt 23.37 which are virtually identical in wording. My translation of a combined version of these two verses is:

> Jerusalem, Jerusalem, you kill the prophets and stone those sent to you! How long did I want to gather your children together just like a bird gathers her chicks under her wings but you weren't willing.

There is some discussion among commentators about the background here.[4] There is a long tradition of linking this passage with Old Testament images of God using female imagery. For example, Jerome (a fourth-century theologian) links it with Deut 32.11 mentioned above.

So it is not difficult to see that the Bible employs a wide range of images for God and that this is also true to a lesser degree when it comes to thinking about Jesus. The question is, what do we make of this when we talk about God and Jesus today? Particularly what do we do about how we preach and how we use words in worship?

A Further Theological Issue

There is quite a discussion amongst biblical and other theological scholars about gendered language for God in the Bible and why the term 'Father' is sometimes used but God is never named as mother. There are a number of issues here to do with the cultural background in which most of the Old Testament, for example, was written—which would sometimes have included female deities. This discussion can be very technical and is not altogether conclusive. Suffice it to say, that the reason why the Old Testament predominantly uses male imagery for God is not because it thinks that God is male—there are other, cultural, factors at play here. It is sometimes argued, partly on the basis of these considerations, that to describe God as 'she' or to use feminine imagery for God is to import a gender reference to God, whereas using the word 'he' to refer to God does not do so. It should be fairly obvious that this is not a logical argument as it assumes that male language is normative and therefore neutral whereas female language is somehow different.

Questions about Language and Gender

2

In most discussions of inclusive language in Christian faith and practice, a distinction is made between language for people and language for God. Most modern theological discussion and liturgical texts avoid using *he, man* and so on generically when they are referring to human beings in general. This is generally uncontroversial nowadays and is not the central subject of this booklet. Gendered language for God is more complicated and is still often controversial. This issue can perhaps be considered in three areas:

- Language for God, including the Trinity;
- Language for Jesus, including the significance of his maleness; and
- Language for the Spirit.

It is one thing to realize that the Bible (and later Christian tradition) talks about God in a variety of ways including feminine imagery but it is another thing to see how this might affect the way we talk about God when we are preaching a sermon, choosing songs and hymns or writing prayers to be used in worship. One helpful factor is that in worship we are often talking to God rather than about God so we can refer to God as *you* rather than always having to use a gendered word like *he* or even *she*.[5]

Language for God

We saw above that the Bible uses a variety of images when talking about God. Some of those who discuss gendered language for God want to maintain that the male images are central and determinative and that all others are secondary. This is not obvious from the biblical material though it is true that in the history of Christian worship the male images have predominated in what is used in material for prayer and worship. Some want to argue that the female images in the Bible are in the form of similes ('God is like a mother bird') whereas the male imagery is in the form of metaphors ('God is our father') and that therefore the male imagery is more real and to be taken literally. This is a fundamental misunderstanding of the nature of simile and metaphor. Both are figures of speech and neither one is more literal than the other. We can see this by using a non-theological example. If I describe my aging vehicle by saying that my car is an old crate, that is a metaphor but if I say that my car is like an old crate that is a simile. Nobody would assume that the first phrase is to be taken literally and the second is not.

More careful theological discussion about language for God will recognize that language for God is always analogical. That is to say, any language we use to describe God is, in the end, an analogy rather than a literal description. This approach preserves the idea that God is other than human by suggesting that human language cannot entirely and completely describe God. We have no option but to use human language to describe God (what else is available?) but we need to remember that this language is limited. It can go so far but cannot define or confine God. Scholars who have discussed these matters have tended to point to four things which we need to bear in mind and which might help us find a way through.

- Ian Ramsey talked about the 'logical oddness' of language about God.[6] In other words, because God is so much greater than we are and so different from us, the use of human language to talk about God will always result in some oddities because human language is not sufficient to the task.
- Ramsey also talked about models and qualifiers when we talk about God. The model is the noun that we might use to describe God, such as rock, king or father. The qualifier is the adjective that we use to modify the meaning of the noun. The reason we need a qualifier is that if we just use a noun that is an everyday image it can sometimes conjure up connections in people's minds that, given reflection, we would not wish to attach to God. To describe God as the king is a good example of this. In the Old Testament, the kings of Israel and Judah were often not brilliant examples of how to be a good and godly leader. When God is described as king, this is meant to evoke ideas such as caring, just and fair rule, not any of the negative things associated with human monarchs. When Jesus calls himself the good shepherd he is using a model and qualifier approach. To have called himself simply the shepherd may have made people think of negative things associated with shepherds as well as positive things.[7] Jesus therefore qualifies 'shepherd' with 'good.' To call God 'Father' raises a similar problem if people have had a bad experience with their own father or if they have grown up in a home where there was not a father. Therefore in *Common Worship* Order One, Eucharistic Prayer D uses the phrase 'Good Father' based on the model of Jesus talking about being the good shepherd.

- Another approach is to say that we cannot say what God is but only what God is not. This is sometimes called the *via negativa*—the negative way (or sometimes apophaticism or the apophatic approach). A further variation on this is to say that in the face of God we can only be silent since human language cannot describe God.
- However, while silence in worship is a valuable thing, the apophatic approach will not help very much when it comes to writing material to use in worship such as prayers and songs and it certainly will not help much with tasks such as preaching and evangelism. The fourth tool is the opposite of this—rich rather than sparse in the use of language. In this approach you use a wide variety of language and imagery for God so that you do not limit God to just a few images. The more images you use, the more faithful you are being to the biblical way of describing God. The technical term for this approach is kataphaticism or the kataphatic approach. Denys Turner named it more accessibly as 'multiplying the names.'[8]

Earlier discussions of the problem of gendered language for God talked about inclusive language. Here the emphasis was often on balancing male imagery with female imagery. This was fine in correcting an exclusive use of masculine language for God but could lead to unhelpful discussions of what the relative percentages should be of masculine and feminine imagery in a given liturgy or text. More recent discussions tend to draw on this but talk about expansive language where the emphasis is on using a broader range of language for God. This goes beyond the gendered language issue and back to the biblical practice of using a wide variety of images for God.

KINGAFAP

Brian Wren, a hymnwriter, points out that, despite the range of biblical images for God, prayers and hymns tend to draw on a limited range of these images which he describes as king, God almighty, father and protector. (He coins the mnemonic KINGAFAP for this.) . Naming the problem in this way is the first step towards doing something about it. Wren therefore is another author who advocates a kataphatic approach to naming God.

Language for the Trinity

A rather more particular problem arises with the standard language used for the Trinity. This is particularly significant in a worship context because we regularly use liturgical texts and hymns with a trinitarian formulae—for instance, creeds, the baptismal formula, blessings, the doxology often used at the end of psalms and canticles, and trinitarian doxological verses at the end of hymns. From early times the trinitarian formula has been 'Father, Son and Holy Spirit.' There have been some attempts to find other formulae. Sally McFague suggests *mother, lover and friend*[9] while David Cunningham suggests *source, wellspring and living water.*[10] Cunningham in particular suggests alternate formulae as supplementing rather than replacing the traditional trinitarian formula. In some places, the formula *creator, redeemer and sustainer* has been used but this is often criticized as allocating particular functions to each person of the Trinity, defining God by what God does rather than who God is.[11] The Church of England's *Common Worship: Daily Prayer* provides this alternative doxology for use at the end of psalms: 'Glory to God, Source of all being, Eternal Word and Holy Spirit…'[12] Gail Ramshaw suggests the way forward would be to expand rather than replace the classic formula and so she suggests using 'Father , Son and Holy Spirit, who is creator, redeemer and sustainer.'[13] This is a good example of expansive language as an approach to the issue of gendered language for God.

Language for Jesus

No one doubts that Jesus was a male human being. However, there are some occasions in the history of Christian spirituality where Jesus is referred to in maternal terms. This takes its cue from biblical texts such as Luke 13.34 and Matt 23.37 discussed above. Perhaps the classic place where this happens is in the *Revelations of Divine Love* of Julian of Norwich. Writing in the late fourteenth century, she speaks of 'Jesus Christ, who…is our true Mother.'[14] (In fact, Julian uses maternal imagery quite a lot and elsewhere describes God as mother and the church as mother. The use of maternal imagery like this was reasonably common in the Middle Ages in English spirituality.)

The early Christian debates about the identity of Jesus which led to doctrinal formulations and creeds affirming that he was fully human and fully divine do not make any theological capital out of Jesus being a male human being. The emphasis is always on the fact that he was human. This is seen most clearly in the original text of the creed produced at the Council of Nicea. This was written originally in Greek and in this language the theological point is made very clearly. A literal translation of the relevant section would read:

> For us humans and for our salvation, he came down from heaven…
> and was made human.

The root word I have translated as humans/human is the Greek word *anthropos*—it is the same word in both places. This is the point that the creed is making here. If you wanted to make it clear in Greek that you were referring to male human beings you would use another word—*aner*.

In other words, in order to save us Jesus became one of us. English translations of the creed do not always make this point clear The international English-language ecumenical version of the creed translates this line of the creed as 'for us and for our salvation, he came down from heaven…and was made truly human.'[15] While the British Methodist Church has adopted this translation, the Church of England refused to do so and has its own unique translation which reads: ' for us and for our salvation, he came down from heaven…and was made man..' This rather unusual generic use of the word *man* (*Common Worship* usually avoids doing this) just causes confusion.[16]

The important thing to make clear in our worship, preaching and evangelism is that Jesus became one of us to save us. In order to be truly human there have to be some particularities. Generally speaking human beings have a particular ethnic background and a particular sexual identity—although nowadays both of these characteristics are seen to be much more complicated than they were a few years ago. Nevertheless, the point is that Jesus became incarnate as a particular human being in order to save all human beings.[17] That is the point the creed is making and nowhere is any particular stress laid on the fact that he was a male saviour.

The Holy Spirit

In many ways, there has been less discussion of gendered language as regards the Holy Spirit. However, comment is often made that the Hebrew word for spirit is feminine (*ruach*).[18] This means that a feminine pronoun will usually be used. However, care is needed here as this is grammatical gender as occurs in many languages though not in English. Thus in French, where every noun must be masculine or feminine, a house is *she* and a garden is *he*. (Except of course a good English translation will use *it* in both cases.) Nevertheless, a custom has grown up of thinking of the Spirit using feminine images (often maternal images). This is sometimes rooted in Gen 1.2 which *The Message* translates as 'God's Spirit brooded like a bird above the watery abyss.'[19]

What are the Issues?

Four general reflections on the theological issues as they apply to worship can be found in the literature on gendered language for God.

- The challenge is to use a wider range of biblical imagery. This is in fact the stated policy of the Church of England Liturgical Commission, as we shall see. *Common Worship* has certainly only partially fulfilled this brief. The British Methodist Church has taken this on board more fully and has made some attempt to use a broader range of imagery, as I discuss in a later chapter.

- This leads to the second common theme in discussion of these issues. Earlier writing talked about gender-inclusive language and focused on replacing male imagery with female imagery. More recent writing uses the phrase expansive language rather than inclusive language. This approach avoids the criticism that inclusive language seeks to make men invisible!
- Ramshaw points out that there is a difference between theological language used in worship and theological language used in discussion and teaching. A key distinction is that in worship we are often talking to God rather than talking about God. This means that when we come to the issue of pronouns in worship we are less concerned with whether we can refer to God as *she* than we are if we were writing a theological essay or even preaching a sermon. In worship we can often use the pronoun *you* when referring to God.
- The fourth issue is whether we should prioritize some images for God over others. Jesus calls God 'Father' so is this to be our main word for describing God? The key thing to remember here is that this father and son language refers to the relationship of Jesus to the father rather than to how either relate to us. Jurgen Moltmann expresses it as 'The Son is the Son of the Father and the Father is the Father of the Son.'[20] We saw that father language for God is rare in the Old Testament and there seems to be less biblical evidence than is sometimes supposed to suggest we should prioritize some images over others as a matter of principle.

3 How Words Work

Many people assume that the relationship between words and the reality they describe is straightforward. We think of something and then we find the words to describe it or express it. However, what the Bible says about the power of words should give us a clue that things are not quite that simple.

There is a long-standing discussion in linguistics about words doing things. At one end of this discussion are the theories put forward by Edward Sapir and Benjamin Whorf. They argued that words create a reality.[21] They went as far as to say that if you speak a language which does not have a word for something, you cannot really conceive of that thing. For example, languages that have a variety of words for different types of snow enable speakers of those languages to have a broader and more varied concept of snow than people who speak a language where there is only one word. Very few people have followed Sapir and Whorf completely in their view that language and words create reality but many people have seen that words do have a power to affect the way we think.

When I was training as a school teacher, one of the pieces of advice I remember being given was that you should never tell a difficult class that they are the worst-behaved pupils you have ever taught because next lesson they surely will be! Likewise, in ministry we might talk up a vision for growth to help people believe it might happen.

Simple descriptions of the relationship between words and reality are seldom entirely true. It is true that we think of something and then we find the words to express it, but it is also true that words can shape the way that we think. The relationship between words and reality is not a one-way street: they affect each other.

Words can shape the way that we think

In terms of language for God, if we always use images for God which are basically male then people might very well (subconsciously) get the idea that God is male whereas if we use a broader variety of images people might get to the idea that God is beyond simple gender identity. If we take the expansive language approach, this will help people to grasp a bigger picture of who God is. Worship is perhaps the most important place where people learn their theology and where their identity as Christians is formed. The ancient Latin phrase attributed to Prosper of Aquitaine, *lex orandi lex credendi*, is often quoted to make this point—it is not quite what Prosper wrote but it sums up what he said and can be translated as 'the law of praying is the law of believing.' The preface to the Church of England's *Alternative Service Book 1980* puts it like this: 'Christians are formed by the way in which they pray, and the way they choose to pray expresses what they are.'[22] This tension between believing and praying matches the tension between words and reality. It is not simply that one shapes the other but rather that they affect each other in a reciprocal way like a cycle. We *are* shaped by the way in which we pray and worship just as much as we find ways of worshipping which express what we believe.

Both the power of words to shape the way we think and understand things and the power of worship to shape us as Christians come together to make it very important that we think about the way in which we talk about God in worship.

What Some Churches Have Said

4

When the British Methodist Church was producing *The Methodist Service Book* in the 1970s and the Church of England was producing *The Alternative Service Book 1980*, the question of gendered language in worship for people, let alone for God, was not really on the agenda. It was a question being raised in North America, both in the Canadian Anglican church and in the Protestant Episcopal church in the USA (as it was then called.)

There was in fact one lone voice on the Church of England Liturgical Commission who was trying to urge that this issue be taken seriously but nobody else on the Commission thought it was important. That person was Jean Mayland. As she said in a speech at General Synod in 1989: '[The ASB] came out just too early, because very soon after its publication these issues began to be taken seriously in our church as they had been taken seriously by the worldwide church before that date.'[23] By the time the ASB was published, it was clear that this was going to be an issue that could no longer be ignored.

Debate and discussion continued in the wider Anglican communion. The 1988 Lambeth Conference discussed inclusive language in worship, including language for God. The Anglican Church in New Zealand produced a new prayer book in 1989 which was innovative in regard to inclusive language and also to inculturation. At the General Convention of the Anglican Church in the USA (ECUSA—now TEC) in 1990, a set of inclusive language liturgies was adopted as a supplement to their 1979 service book. Interestingly (for comparison with the Church of England's own position), the preface to this supplemental book states:

> ...language referring to the human community should express inclusivity in all instances. For example, masculine pronouns are no longer used in phrases of general human reference. Regarding language used in reference to God, the primary concern has been that of fidelity to biblical language. The biblical metaphors of Father and Lord have a fundamental place in Christian prayer and theology and have been retained, although their use is less frequent than in existing *Prayer Book* services. Other scriptural images of God, including feminine images from the Wisdom literature, have been introduced.[24]

This is almost the same as the policy later adopted by the Church of England's Liturgical Commission (discussed below) except that it specifies where the feminine imagery is to come from.

The Church of England

The Church of England began to address the issue of gendered language in its 1985 report *The Worship of the Church.*[25] Inclusive language is listed as one of three issues concerning the language of worship. The comment is tellingly brief and is as follows:

> Secondly, there is the matter of inclusive language, a principle which (although it may have many applications across age, ethnic, class and intelligence barriers) is usually invoked in relation to the apparent 'male-ness' of the English generic terms for the human race ('to love and serve all men,' etc). The present Liturgical Commission sees this as a 'problem' which will not go away, and needs to be solved by a sensitive recasting of offending passages. The Commission does not share the view sometimes heard that male pronouns and possessive adjectives in relation to God are inappropriate, and on that issue simply wishes to conform to scriptural and traditional usage. It does, however, consider that the general issue requires serious and continuing attention by the next Commission and, in due course (and in the light of the Commission's work), by the House of Bishops and by the Synod.[26]

It is interesting to note that the Commission refers to inclusive language as a problem to be solved and not as an opportunity to be grasped. It is also significant that it is very wary of inclusive language with regard to God and speaks of scriptural usage, apparently unaware of biblical passages using non-masculine imagery for God. Subsequent reports by the Liturgical Commission have taken much the same line, even though the Commission's membership has changed. It is possible to see later developments such as *Common Worship* as echoing the sentiments of this 1985 report, which shows consistency but reveals that the insights of inclusive language have not been fully taken on board.

An Unofficial Contribution

In 1986, Grove Books published *Count Us In! Inclusive Language in Liturgy* by Jane Sinclair and Viv Faull in the Liturgical Studies series.[27] This was the first extensive and accessible discussion of the issue in UK and remained so for some years.[28]

In 1988 the Liturgical Commission published its report *Making Women Visible* as a response to the 1985 report and the subsequent Synod debate on it.[29] The debate came about because by 1988 a substantial number of Synod members had signed in support of a Private Member's Motion calling for a debate on it.

Making Women Visible begins with a summary of the linguistic and theological issues involved with inclusive language for people. The method of the chapter is to state the opposing cases and leave it there. The authors who were used to illustrate opposition to inclusive language do not actually engage with the arguments of those who advocate it.

Making Women Visible goes on to suggest alternatives to generic male language and to offer a few new texts as samples, some of which are taken up by later Liturgical Commission works. This report can be said to have shaped inclusive language in the Church of England.

The report does not address gendered language for God except in the Nicene Creed where it ducks the issue in a bizarre *volte face*. The argument against seeing 'man' as generic is reasonably forcefully made and would lead the reader to think that the creed would be retranslated to use the word 'human,' especially as the report acknowledges that 'and was made man' does not accurately represent what the original text of the creed is trying to say. The Anglo-Orthodox Society had proposed 'and was made human' and the report notes that 'and became human' could be argued as being equally acceptable. However, in the end, the Liturgical Commission (along with the ecumenical Joint Liturgical Group) responded to the ELLC proposals by arguing for the retention of 'and was made man.' The reason given in *Making Women Visible* is that the change would involve the 'loss of a familiar phrase.' The argument therefore turns on euphony and familiarity rather than theology and accuracy.

In preparation for the revision of the ASB which became *Common Worship*, the Liturgical Commission produced a report in 1994 called 'Language and the Worship of the Church' (GS 1115). It began with a discussion of theological issues around the way language works but this is very brief and has no references to the wider literature. After a discussion of the relative merits of the language of the BCP and that of the ASB, the report the devotes four paragraphs to gender-inclusive language in general terms. Here it notes that debate has moved on since *Making Women Visible* to include inclusive language for God as a more pressing issue than was seen in 1988. Four issues are highlighted:

- the use of predominantly male images for God;
- the use of male pronouns for God;

- the fact that trinitarian references and formulae pose the most complex questions;
- while references to God as 'being part of a male hierarchy' are unacceptable in some cultures they are part and parcel of others.

This report then offers some guidelines for future liturgical revision (that is, the project that became *Common Worship*). In essence these are that it is often difficult to change historic texts and that there is no compulsion to do so but that texts being written from scratch should use gender-inclusive language for people and should use a wide range of images for God 'especially those drawn from Scripture.'[30]

In September 2011 the then Archbishop of Canterbury, Rowan Williams, convened a meeting of about 60 people at Lambeth Palace to consider the impact of the ordination of women on the Church of England and what issues needed now to be addressed regarding gender equality. Janet Morley and I led a seminar on inclusive language in worship as part of this consultation. One of the outcomes of this day was to set up the *Transformations* project in part to look at what further work needed to be done on inclusive language in worship. The Liturgical Commission is currently considering the topic of gender in relation to how we name God in collaboration with the Faith and Order Commission. Until fairly recently in its work, it has not been clear how this current discussion has worked with what has been written before by the Liturgical Commission about this.

British Methodism

In contrast to the rather tortuous series of debates in the Church of England (not all of which I have described in the section above), the British Methodist Church has had a much more straightforward discussion about gender inclusive language in liturgy. It has produced the fullest and most helpful policy document in the 1992 report to the Methodist Conference 'Inclusive Language and Imagery about God.'

The report begins with some general background discussion, first of all about the way in which the English language has developed and how forms which might once have been heard as inclusive (such as the generic use of words like *man*) are not heard that way any more. This section also shows how the English language has often been more gender inclusive in the past than people think. There is then a discussion of a second introductory issue, namely theological issues around imagery for God. Here the report draws on a wider range of theological resources than do reports in other churches. Other introductory sections deal with the diversity of biblical imagery for God and the pastoral and missiological implications of how we describe God.

This report then concludes with some recommendations for action, which include some sample texts, and a summary of why this whole issue is important and what the church's responses to it might be. A summary of this last section is worth noting—the three possible responses are:

- replace male imagery with female imagery (but this raises as many questions as it solves);
- eliminate all gendered imagery (but this cuts us off from rich spiritual resources);
- balance male and female imagery in creative tension. (This last is what is recommended.)

However, it will be noted that this set of proposals goes back to an approach which focuses on gendered language rather than the expansive language approach which I have been advocating.

5 What Some Churches Have Done

Most modern language service books in English-speaking countries have adopted gender-inclusive language for people. Some have explored expansive language for God. There are often more texts using expansive language available than service planners and leaders realize, so that much useful material goes unused and the result is that congregations get a restricted diet as far as imagery for God goes.

Describing God

One clear example of using a broader range of images for God comes from the collects in the Church of England's *Common Worship* provision. The original collects provided for *Common Worship* were widely criticized as being complicated in language and lengthy (and some times archaic) in structure. An additional set of shorter and simpler collects was produced.[31] This alternative set uses a broader range of imagery for God in the opening line. An example would be to compare the two collects provided for the 9th Sunday after Trinity. The original collect begins:

> Almighty God,
> who sent your Holy Spirit
> to be the life and light of your Church…

While the alternative collect begins:

> Gracious Father…

The alternative in this case does of course retain the naming of God as Father but a comparison of the opening descriptions for God in the two sets of collects reveals the following information. In the original set of collects the following descriptions of God are used:

Description of God	*Frequency of Use*	*Approximate Percentage of Use*
Almighty God	36	42
Eternal	12	14
Lord	9	11

Father	8	9
[O] God	7	8
Merciful	4	5
Redeemer	2	2

Seven other descriptions are used once each.

The same data from the additional collects is as follows:

Description of God	*Frequency of Use*	*Approximate Percentage of Use*
Almighty God	9	13
Father/Heavenly Father etc.	8	11
Risen Christ	6	9
Eternal God/Lord	4	6
Creator	4	6
God of all mercy etc.	4	6
Holy God/God of holiness	4	6
God of glory	3	4
Lord God	3	4
Lord Jesus Christ	2	3
God the only/our saviour	2	3

Twenty-one other descriptions are used once each.

Even a quick glance at the two tables shows that the additional collects use a broader range of imagery for God because there are simply more entries on the list. The percentage describing God as almighty has reduced but the percentage of describing God as Father has slightly increased. (In this discussion I am assuming that 'almighty' is generally heard as a masculine image, but this is open to debate.)

Another place where the Church of England has experimented with a wider range of ways of addressing God is in the prayers provided for each of the psalms in *Common Worship: Daily Prayer*. While not designed to address gender issues specifically, they do incorporate a wider range of addresses to God than is typical in liturgical resources (for instance, 'Holy God'; 'Strong and gracious God'; 'Faithful and steadfast God'; 'God our deliverer').

This approach, which I have named in this booklet as expansive language, is a relatively simple approach to use. The Methodist Church does this in many of its additional eucharistic prayers where, for example in the Advent service, different paragraphs begin with different ways of naming God:[32]

- the God of all creation;
- loving God;
- gracious God.

before concluding with a trinitarian congregational text which uses Father, Son and Holy Spirit.

Another prayer in this collection uses:

- Redeeming God;
- Faithful God;
- Creator God;
- Loving God.

Divine Pronouns

Another issue is the use of pronouns to refer to God. Biblical texts in their original languages always use masculine pronouns. This is largely to do with the fact that the words for God are themselves grammatically masculine. Modern liturgical texts in churches such as the Methodist Church and the Church of England continue to use male pronouns to refer to God but there are ways of reducing the frequency with which this happens and therefore reducing the overall impression of God being male. A common example of this comes in the Peruvian Gloria. This is a song, not a liturgical text, but the change which is commonly made illustrates this point. The original text is:

Glory to God, glory to God, glory to the Father....
To him be glory forever.

However, this is routinely changed in many hymn books to:

Glory to God, glory to God, glory to the Father....
To God be glory forever.

It is often easy to use the word God instead of a male pronoun although this cannot be done too frequently or else it becomes repetitive and jarring. In the opening part of the eucharistic prayer, often known by its Latin name the *Sursum Corda*, the final section which reads (for example in *The Alternative Service Book 1980*):[33]

Let us give thanks to the Lord our God.
It is right to give him thanks and praise.

now reads (in *Common Worship*)

Let us give thanks to the Lord our God.
It is right to give thanks and praise.

This is in fact a more accurate version of the original text which arose in a Latin speaking culture and where the text just said *'Dignum et justum est'* ('It is fitting and just'). In other words, the Latin original does not have a gendered pronoun here and it was modern language liturgy which put one in. This is a good example of where more recent revisions have become less gendered by going back to a more literal translation of the original.

The *Methodist Worship Book* has a different text at this point and reads:

Let us give thanks to the Lord our God.
It is right to give our thanks and praise.

This keeps the same number of words as the earlier version but removes the gendered pronoun. However it changes the focus by including the word *our*. In this version there is more focus on what *we* are doing rather than on what God is worthy to receive.

Language evolves and changes. A current complex and developing issue is what to do with replacing 'himself' in relation to God. 'Godself' can be used, but at present it tends to sound odd, or at least a little forced. However, language changes which seem radical or eccentric when they start can eventually become normalized.

It may also be that current controversies about gender in relation to human beings may give us new ways of using pronouns for God that are personal, without being gendered. Using 'they/them' as individual pronouns has more historical precedent than is often realized and is commonly used as an indefinite pronoun as in 'If someone came to church, they would meet Jesus.' This does not transfer easily to talking about God but in years to come this aspect of English may work differently.

Language for Jesus

There are two places in *Common Worship* where a more expansive use of language about Jesus can be found. One is in Eucharistic Prayer G which picks up Jesus' prayer over Jerusalem in Luke 13 and Matthew 23:

How wonderful the work of your hands, O Lord.
As a mother tenderly gathers her children,
you embraced a people as your own.

However, the eucharistic prayer is speaking to God rather than to Jesus, so the biblical reference lying behind this particular text is not simply the words of Jesus but also, much more obliquely, a text such as Hosea 11 where God is depicted as a parent.

The other place in *Common Worship* where feminine language for Jesus is used is in a canticle, *A Song of Anselm*:

Jesus, like a mother you gather your people to you;
you are gentle with us as a mother with her children.

This picks up the lament of Jesus over Jerusalem very clearly.

As noted above, although the Church of England declined to adopt the ELLC version of the Nicene Creed, the Methodist Church has adopted it and so has 'and became truly human.'

Spirit and Trinity

Neither the Church of England nor the Methodist Church has adopted expansive language in naming the Spirit or the Trinity but the hymn *She Sits like a Bird* by John Bell and Graham Maule does pick up the idea of the Spirit as a nurturing bird (and refers to the Spirit as *she* throughout):[34]

She sits like a bird, brooding on the waters,
Hovering on the chaos of the world's first day.

And later the hymn refers to the coming of the Spirit at Pentecost:

She dances in fire, startling her spectators,
Waking tongues of ecstasy where dumbness reigned…

Some Things We Can Do Now 6

Perhaps this booklet has made you aware of ways in which worship in your church—perhaps worship in which you have a leadership role—could be reinforcing gendered ideas about God which are not true to who God really is. We have seen that some denominations are moving (sometimes slowly) to address this in their formal liturgy. In the meantime, this chapter suggests some things that can be done in a local church.

Audit Your Worship

Any church can audit its worship with regard to language for God. Have a look at some services in your church and see what images are used for God. Do not forget to include things like hymns and prayers alongside the authorized texts (if your church uses centrally-produced texts). Remember to analyze which of the centrally-produced texts you use and which never get used. You might also include the sermon. You can try to classify the images or descriptions of God to see whether your worship leans towards one set of images more than others. This is where a tool such as Brian Wren's KINGAFAP can be useful (see chapter two) but remember that all tools can be blunt instruments. The point of this exercise is to get a general idea about whether, in your worship, you are using a good range of biblical images for God or whether you tend to focus on one type. You might refine your analysis by seeing whether the images for God used in hymns and songs are different from those used in the set liturgy or preaching.

Study and Discuss the Issue

You could also have some home groups, study groups or even sermons looking at images for God in the Bible. People might be quite surprised at what a wide range there is and this could lead to a discussion about how we use this material in worship. You could even have a go at writing new material for worship which could include things that you sing as well as spoken prayer texts.

Explore Your Church's Official Material

There is a lot of creative material in the Church of England's *Common Worship* and in the Methodist Church's resources. However, you have to go hunting for much of this, especially in *Common Worship*. There are quickly discoverable *Common Worship* resources in the set of Additional Collects and Psalm Prayers mentioned above. Using these collects rather than the original ones will instantly expand language used for naming God. A look at the Psalm Prayers can also provide inspiration for your own prayers.

Some Other Quick Wins

Some easy changes you can make when writing your own prayers, or praying extempore are as follows.

- Try to avoid, or reduce, constant use of male pronouns for God. You can sometimes do this by replacing 'his' with 'God's.' You might sometimes need to rephrase the sentence (for instance, 'Let's thank God for his love and mercy' could become 'Let's give thanks for God's love and mercy').
- Look for opportunities for addressing God rather than talking about God (this means 'you' replaces 'he/him').
- Vary how you start your prayers (take the ideas from denominational liturgies mentioned earlier in the booklet and apply them to your extempore praying).
- Vary how you end your prayers. For instance, try praying 'through Jesus Christ our Saviour,' rather than always 'through Jesus Christ our Lord.'

When leaders make changes to how they pray and talk about God in church services, it can start to shape how other Christians pray in small groups and in their own personal prayers. Anglican ministers might want to remember that these are changes that might be possible even in authorized liturgical texts, under the provisions of Canon B5.[35]

Divine Pronouns on Screen and in Print

When it is not possible to change male pronouns for God, make sure that the way they are presented does not make their impact even worse. Some song-projection software, and some printed resources, tend to capitalize pronouns that relate to God ('Praise my soul…to His feet thy tribute bring'). This has the effect of drawing attention to the pronoun, making them more prominent. English Bible translations do not capitalize pronouns for God, so there is no need to do it in songs and hymns.

Choosing and Amending Songs and Hymns

If a song or hymn has a very dominantly male set of pronouns, addresses or descriptions relating to God, then it might be worth considering if there is something else we could sing instead which does the same job without the problems. If a hymn is out of copyright, it might be possible to make some of the changes suggested above (though be careful if it is well-known and changes are likely to trip people up). The safest approach might be to tell people up front that you are trying a new approach with the hymn, explaining why, and inviting them to reflect on how it affects the way they think of God.

Notes

1 The technical term here is linguistic determinism, associated with the American linguistics scholars Edward Sapir and Benjamin Whorf. There is a huge discussion of this but a good starting point focusing on gender remains D Spender's *Man Made Language* (London: Routledge and Kegan Paul, 1980).

2 P Tovey, *Praying to God as Mother* (Grove Spirituality booklet S 38) p 5.

3 For example, J D G Dunn, *Christology in the Making* (London: SCM, 1980).

4 C F Evans, *St Luke* (London: SCM, 1990) has a succinct discussion of much of the background and other issues.

5 A point made by Gail Ramshaw among others—see her *God Beyond Gender* (Minneapolis, MN: Fortress, 1995) for a helpful discussion of this and other matters covered in this booklet.

6 I Ramsey, *Religious Language* (London: SCM, 1957).

7 It is often alleged that first-century shepherds had a bad reputation and were unreliable. This is disputed but might have some truth in it—see K Bailey, *Poet and Peasant* (Grand Rapids, MI: Eerdmans, 1976) p 147.

8 In his 1993 Alan Richardson lecture at the University of Durham entitled 'Atheism, Mysticism and Mystification: How to Tell the Difference.'

9 S McFague, *Models for God* (London: SCM, 1987).

10 D Cunningham, *These Three are One* (Oxford: Blackwell, 1997).

11 This is usually named as the ancient heresy of modalism, though it does not have to be modalistic.

12 *Common Worship: Daily Prayer* (London: Church House Publishing, 2005) p 648, Note 3.

13 G Ramshaw, 'In the Name' in *The Ecumenical Review* 54.3 (2002).

14 E College and J Walsh, *Julian of Norwich: Showings* (New York: Paulist Press, 1978) p 295.

15 Known as ELLC—English Language Liturgical Consultation

16 I moved an amendment in General Synod that the Church of England should adopt the ELLC version but I was not successful.

17 For the avoidance of doubt I am not suggesting that this implies universal salvation but I do think it implies that the offer of salvation is made to everybody—to

use the formulation often found in Methodist discussions, all need to be saved and all can be saved.

18 The Hebrew word *nephesh* is also sometimes translated *spirit* but this is in the sense of a human being, not the Spirit of God.

19 It should be noted that this verse contains several translation difficulties—the word often translated 'Spirit' can also be 'wind' or 'breath' and the word translated 'brooded' could be 'hovered' or 'swept.' See how other translations such as NIV, NRSV and AV translate this.

20 For example, J Moltmann, 'The Motherly Father: Is Trinitarian Patripassianism Replacing Theological Patriarchalism?' in Concilium 1981 vol 3.

21 Se *eg* D Cameron, *Feminism and Linguistic Theory* (London: Macmillan, 1985) especially pp 134–138.

22 The *Alternative Service Book 1980* (London: SPCK *et al*, 1980) p 10.

23 It was Jean herself who told me about this in several conversations when we were working together on gender-equality issues about 20 years ago. Her General Synod speech is in *General Synod Report of Proceedings* July 1989 p 512.

24 ECUSA Supplemental Liturgical Texts (Church Hymnal Corporation, 1989) p 6.

25 GS 698—the Standing Committee of the General Synod published this report, based largely on a report by the Liturgical Commission produced for the Standing Committee, which assesses the impact of the ASB in the five years since its introduction and looks to future areas of development in the worship of the church.

26 GS 698 pp 14f.

27 This was a more academically-oriented series which has now become the Joint Liturgical Studies published by Hymns Ancient and Modern and produced by the Group for the Renewal of Worship and the Alcuin Club jointly—see https://www.hymnsam.co.uk/joint-liturgical-studies/

28 Subsequent reports like 'Making Women Visible' (from the Church of England) and 'Inclusive Language and Imagery about God' (from the British Methodist Church) do not provide such an extensive discussion of the issues.

29 GS 859.

30 *Making Women Visible* remains the overarching policy document and it is suggested that studies should be made of the use of gender-inclusive language in the Church of England's worship.

31 *Common Worship: Additional Collects* were originally published online and in a separate booklet. They have now been incorporated in the second edition of the *Common Worship* main volume (2024).

32 *Additional Orders of Holy Communion* (supplementary to those in the *Methodist Worship Book*) at https://media.methodist.org.uk/media/documents/additional-holy-communion-20221215.pdf

33 Which means 'Lift up your hearts'—see C Read, *Understanding the Eucharistic Prayer* (Grove Worship booklet W 253).

34 J L Bell and Graham Maule © 1988, WGRG, Iona Community.

35 Canon B5 allows for the minister to make 'variations which are not of substantial importance,' as long as they are 'reverent and seemly' and 'neither contrary to, nor indicative of any departure from, the doctrine of the Church of England in any essential matter.'